50 Creative Sandwich Ideas

By: Kelly Johnson

Table of Contents

- Avocado and Egg Breakfast Sandwich
- Caprese Sandwich with Mozzarella, Tomato, and Basil
- Spicy Sriracha Chicken Sandwich
- Grilled Cheese with Tomato and Bacon
- Falafel Pita Sandwich
- Smoked Salmon and Cream Cheese Bagel
- BBQ Pulled Pork Sandwich
- Vegan Chickpea Salad Sandwich
- Chicken Caesar Wrap
- Turkey and Cranberry Sauce Sandwich
- Roasted Veggie and Hummus Sandwich
- Cuban Sandwich with Ham, Pork, Swiss, and Pickles
- Eggplant Parmesan Sandwich
- Peanut Butter, Banana, and Honey Sandwich
- Steak and Caramelized Onion Sandwich
- Grilled Portobello Mushroom Sandwich
- Chicken Parmesan Sandwich
- Tuna Salad Sandwich
- Buffalo Chicken and Blue Cheese Sandwich
- Meatball Sub with Marinara and Mozzarella
- Pesto and Mozzarella Grilled Cheese
- Pastrami and Swiss Rye Sandwich
- Falafel and Tzatziki Flatbread
- Sweet Potato and Black Bean Sandwich
- Banh Mi with Pork, Pickled Veggies, and Cilantro
- Turkey, Brie, and Apple Sandwich
- Roasted Beet and Goat Cheese Sandwich
- Crispy Chicken and Coleslaw Sandwich
- BBQ Jackfruit Sandwich (Vegan Pulled Pork)
- Grilled Shrimp Po' Boy Sandwich
- Sweet and Spicy Meatball Sandwich
- Veggie and Hummus Wrap
- Shrimp Avocado Sandwich
- Roasted Turkey and Spinach Pita
- Grilled Veggie and Goat Cheese Sandwich

- Salmon Salad Sandwich
- Brie, Pear, and Arugula Sandwich
- Cucumber and Cream Cheese Sandwich
- Chicken and Waffle Sandwich
- Veggie and Avocado Wrap
- Ham, Egg, and Cheese Croissant Sandwich
- Chicken and Pesto Panini
- Buffalo Cauliflower Wrap
- Apple and Cheddar Sandwich
- Bacon, Lettuce, and Tomato Sandwich (BLT)
- Sweet Chili Chicken Sandwich
- Roasted Garlic and Tomato Sandwich
- Mediterranean Veggie Wrap
- Grilled Cheese with Fig Jam and Prosciutto
- Hummus and Avocado Toast Sandwich

Avocado and Egg Breakfast Sandwich

Ingredients:

- 1 ripe avocado, mashed
- 1 egg
- 1 whole grain English muffin, toasted
- Salt and pepper, to taste
- 1 tablespoon olive oil
- Optional: hot sauce or salsa

Instructions:

1. Heat olive oil in a pan over medium heat. Crack the egg into the pan and cook to your desired doneness (fried, scrambled, or poached).
2. While the egg cooks, spread mashed avocado on the toasted English muffin.
3. Once the egg is cooked, place it on top of the avocado.
4. Season with salt, pepper, and optional hot sauce or salsa. Serve immediately.

Caprese Sandwich with Mozzarella, Tomato, and Basil

Ingredients:

- 2 slices of fresh ciabatta bread
- 2 large slices of fresh mozzarella cheese
- 2-3 slices of ripe tomato
- Fresh basil leaves
- Balsamic glaze
- Salt and pepper, to taste
- Olive oil (optional)

Instructions:

1. Arrange the mozzarella slices on one piece of ciabatta bread.
2. Layer the tomato slices and basil leaves on top.
3. Drizzle with balsamic glaze and olive oil, then season with salt and pepper.
4. Top with the second slice of bread, cut in half, and serve.

Spicy Sriracha Chicken Sandwich

Ingredients:

- 1 grilled chicken breast
- 2 slices of your favorite bread (brioche, whole wheat, etc.)
- 1 tablespoon Sriracha sauce
- 2 tablespoons mayonnaise
- Lettuce or spinach
- Tomato slices
- Salt and pepper, to taste

Instructions:

1. Mix Sriracha and mayonnaise to create the spicy sauce.
2. Spread the sauce on one side of each slice of bread.
3. Place the grilled chicken breast on one slice of bread.
4. Top with lettuce, tomato slices, and season with salt and pepper.
5. Close the sandwich and serve immediately.

Grilled Cheese with Tomato and Bacon

Ingredients:

- 2 slices of bread (sourdough, white, or whole wheat)
- 2 slices of cheddar cheese
- 2-3 slices of cooked bacon
- 1 tomato, sliced
- 1 tablespoon butter

Instructions:

1. Butter one side of each slice of bread.
2. Place one slice of bread, butter-side down, in a skillet over medium heat.
3. Add cheese, bacon, and tomato slices.
4. Top with the second slice of bread, butter-side up.
5. Grill for 3-4 minutes on each side, until golden brown and cheese is melted.
6. Slice in half and serve warm.

Falafel Pita Sandwich

Ingredients:

- 4-5 falafel balls (store-bought or homemade)
- 1 whole pita bread
- Hummus or tahini sauce
- Cucumber, sliced
- Tomato, sliced
- Lettuce
- Red onion, thinly sliced

Instructions:

1. Warm the pita bread and cut it open to create a pocket.
2. Spread a generous amount of hummus or tahini sauce inside.
3. Add the falafel balls, followed by cucumber, tomato, lettuce, and red onion.
4. Serve immediately, and enjoy the fresh flavors!

Smoked Salmon and Cream Cheese Bagel

Ingredients:

- 1 bagel, sliced
- 2-3 ounces smoked salmon
- 2 tablespoons cream cheese
- 1 tablespoon capers
- Red onion, thinly sliced
- Fresh dill, for garnish
- Lemon wedges

Instructions:

1. Toast the bagel halves until golden brown.
2. Spread cream cheese on each half of the bagel.
3. Layer smoked salmon on top of the cream cheese.
4. Add capers, red onion slices, and garnish with fresh dill.
5. Serve with a squeeze of lemon juice.

BBQ Pulled Pork Sandwich

Ingredients:

- 1 cup pulled pork (cooked and shredded)
- 1 tablespoon BBQ sauce
- 2 slices of brioche or sandwich buns
- Coleslaw (optional)
- Pickles (optional)

Instructions:

1. Mix the pulled pork with BBQ sauce in a bowl.
2. Heat the pork in a pan or microwave until warmed through.
3. Place the pulled pork on the bottom half of the bun.
4. Top with coleslaw and pickles, if desired.
5. Close the sandwich and serve.

Vegan Chickpea Salad Sandwich

Ingredients:

- 1 can chickpeas, drained and mashed
- 2 tablespoons vegan mayo
- 1 tablespoon mustard
- 1 tablespoon lemon juice
- Salt and pepper, to taste
- 2 slices whole wheat or gluten-free bread
- Lettuce, tomato, and cucumber slices

Instructions:

1. Mash the chickpeas in a bowl and mix with vegan mayo, mustard, lemon juice, salt, and pepper.
2. Spread the chickpea salad on one slice of bread.
3. Top with lettuce, tomato, and cucumber slices.
4. Place the second slice of bread on top, slice in half, and serve.

Chicken Caesar Wrap

Ingredients:

- 1 grilled chicken breast, sliced
- 1 large flour tortilla
- 1/2 cup Caesar dressing
- 1 cup Romaine lettuce, chopped
- 2 tablespoons grated Parmesan cheese
- Croutons (optional)

Instructions:

1. Warm the tortilla slightly in a pan or microwave.
2. In a large bowl, toss the sliced chicken with Caesar dressing, Romaine lettuce, and Parmesan cheese.
3. Lay the mixture in the center of the tortilla and top with croutons if desired.
4. Fold the sides of the tortilla over the filling and roll it up tightly.
5. Slice in half and serve.

Turkey and Cranberry Sauce Sandwich

Ingredients:

- 2 slices of whole grain or sourdough bread
- 3-4 ounces sliced turkey breast
- 2 tablespoons cranberry sauce
- Lettuce (optional)
- Salt and pepper to taste

Instructions:

1. Spread cranberry sauce on one slice of bread.
2. Layer the sliced turkey on top of the sauce.
3. Add lettuce if desired, and season with salt and pepper.
4. Top with the second slice of bread and serve.

Roasted Veggie and Hummus Sandwich

Ingredients:

- 2 slices whole wheat bread
- 1/2 cup hummus
- 1/2 cup roasted vegetables (such as bell peppers, zucchini, and eggplant)
- Spinach or arugula
- Salt and pepper to taste

Instructions:

1. Spread hummus on both slices of bread.
2. Layer the roasted vegetables on one slice of bread.
3. Add spinach or arugula and season with salt and pepper.
4. Top with the second slice of bread and serve.

Cuban Sandwich with Ham, Pork, Swiss, and Pickles

Ingredients:

- 1 Cuban roll or baguette
- 3-4 slices ham
- 3-4 slices roast pork
- 2 slices Swiss cheese
- 4-5 pickle slices
- Mustard (optional)

Instructions:

1. Slice the Cuban roll lengthwise and spread mustard (if using) on the inside.
2. Layer the ham, roast pork, Swiss cheese, and pickle slices.
3. Close the sandwich and press it on a panini press or grill it on a skillet until the cheese melts and the bread is crispy.
4. Slice and serve warm.

Eggplant Parmesan Sandwich

Ingredients:

- 2 slices of Italian bread or a sub roll
- 1 eggplant, sliced into rounds
- 1/2 cup marinara sauce
- 1/2 cup mozzarella cheese, shredded
- 2 tablespoons Parmesan cheese, grated
- Olive oil for frying

Instructions:

1. Heat olive oil in a pan and fry the eggplant slices until golden brown and crispy.
2. Toast the bread or sub roll in the oven or on a skillet.
3. Layer the fried eggplant on one slice of bread and top with marinara sauce and mozzarella.
4. Sprinkle Parmesan cheese over the top.
5. Top with the second slice of bread, slice, and serve.

Peanut Butter, Banana, and Honey Sandwich

Ingredients:

- 2 slices whole wheat or multigrain bread
- 2 tablespoons peanut butter
- 1 banana, sliced
- 1 tablespoon honey

Instructions:

1. Spread peanut butter on one slice of bread.
2. Layer the banana slices on top of the peanut butter.
3. Drizzle honey over the banana slices.
4. Top with the second slice of bread and serve.

Steak and Caramelized Onion Sandwich

Ingredients:

- 1 steak (ribeye or sirloin), cooked to your liking and thinly sliced
- 2 slices of toasted baguette or sandwich roll
- 1/2 cup caramelized onions
- 1 tablespoon Dijon mustard (optional)

Instructions:

1. Slice the cooked steak thinly.
2. Spread Dijon mustard on one slice of the bread if desired.
3. Layer the sliced steak and caramelized onions on the bread.
4. Top with the second slice of bread and serve immediately.

Grilled Portobello Mushroom Sandwich

Ingredients:

- 1 large Portobello mushroom cap, cleaned and stems removed
- 1 tablespoon olive oil
- 1 clove garlic, minced
- 2 slices whole grain or sourdough bread
- Lettuce or spinach
- Tomato slices
- Balsamic glaze (optional)

Instructions:

1. Brush the Portobello mushroom cap with olive oil and sprinkle with minced garlic, salt, and pepper.
2. Grill the mushroom on each side for 4-5 minutes until tender.
3. Toast the bread slices and layer with lettuce or spinach, grilled mushroom, and tomato slices.
4. Drizzle with balsamic glaze if desired, then top with the second slice of bread and serve.

Chicken Parmesan Sandwich

Ingredients:

- 2 slices Italian bread or sub roll
- 1 breaded chicken breast, fried or baked
- 1/2 cup marinara sauce
- 1/2 cup mozzarella cheese, shredded
- 2 tablespoons Parmesan cheese, grated
- Fresh basil leaves (optional)

Instructions:

1. Toast the bread or sub roll slices.
2. Place the breaded chicken breast on one slice of the bread.
3. Spoon marinara sauce over the chicken, then top with mozzarella and Parmesan cheese.
4. Broil or bake in the oven until the cheese is melted and bubbly.
5. Top with fresh basil leaves if desired and serve.

Tuna Salad Sandwich

Ingredients:

- 2 slices whole grain or white bread
- 1 can tuna, drained
- 2 tablespoons mayonnaise
- 1 tablespoon Dijon mustard
- 1 tablespoon chopped red onion
- 1 tablespoon chopped celery
- Salt and pepper to taste

Instructions:

1. In a bowl, combine the tuna, mayonnaise, mustard, red onion, and celery.
2. Season with salt and pepper.
3. Spread the tuna salad onto one slice of bread.
4. Top with the second slice of bread and serve.

Buffalo Chicken and Blue Cheese Sandwich

Ingredients:

- 2 slices bread (such as whole wheat or a sub roll)
- 1 grilled or shredded chicken breast
- 1/4 cup buffalo sauce
- 1/4 cup blue cheese crumbles
- Lettuce or spinach (optional)

Instructions:

1. Toss the chicken with buffalo sauce.
2. Layer the saucy chicken on one slice of bread.
3. Sprinkle blue cheese crumbles over the chicken.
4. Add lettuce or spinach for some crunch if desired.
5. Top with the second slice of bread and serve.

Meatball Sub with Marinara and Mozzarella

Ingredients:

- 1 sub roll or Italian baguette
- 4-5 meatballs, cooked
- 1/2 cup marinara sauce
- 1/2 cup mozzarella cheese, shredded
- Fresh basil or parsley (optional)

Instructions:

1. Warm the meatballs in marinara sauce.
2. Slice the sub roll and toast it lightly.
3. Place the meatballs into the roll, spooning sauce over them.
4. Sprinkle mozzarella cheese over the meatballs and broil until the cheese melts.
5. Top with fresh basil or parsley, then serve.

Pesto and Mozzarella Grilled Cheese

Ingredients:

- 2 slices sourdough bread
- 1 tablespoon pesto
- 2 slices mozzarella cheese
- 1 tablespoon butter

Instructions:

1. Spread pesto on one side of each slice of bread.
2. Place the mozzarella cheese between the two slices of bread, pesto side in.
3. Butter the outside of the bread.
4. Grill the sandwich on a skillet over medium heat until golden brown and the cheese is melted.
5. Slice and serve.

Pastrami and Swiss Rye Sandwich

Ingredients:

- 2 slices rye bread
- 4-5 slices pastrami
- 2 slices Swiss cheese
- 1 tablespoon mustard
- Pickles (optional)

Instructions:

1. Spread mustard on one slice of rye bread.
2. Layer the pastrami and Swiss cheese on top.
3. Add pickles if desired.
4. Top with the second slice of rye bread and serve.

Falafel and Tzatziki Flatbread

Ingredients:

- 1 flatbread or pita
- 4-5 falafel balls, warmed
- 1/4 cup tzatziki sauce
- Sliced cucumber and tomato
- Fresh parsley

Instructions:

1. Warm the flatbread or pita.
2. Place the falafel balls on the flatbread.
3. Drizzle tzatziki sauce over the falafel and top with cucumber, tomato, and parsley.
4. Roll or fold the flatbread and serve.

Sweet Potato and Black Bean Sandwich

Ingredients:

- 2 slices whole wheat bread
- 1 small sweet potato, roasted and mashed
- 1/2 cup black beans, rinsed and drained
- 1/4 avocado, sliced
- Salt and pepper to taste

Instructions:

1. Mash the roasted sweet potato and season with salt and pepper.
2. Layer the mashed sweet potato on one slice of bread.
3. Add black beans and avocado slices.
4. Top with the second slice of bread and serve.

Banh Mi with Pork, Pickled Veggies, and Cilantro

Ingredients:

- 1 baguette
- 1/2 cup cooked pork (shredded or sliced)
- 1/4 cup pickled carrots and daikon radish
- Fresh cilantro leaves
- Cucumber, thinly sliced
- 1 tablespoon mayonnaise
- 1 teaspoon sriracha (optional)
- Soy sauce for drizzling

Instructions:

1. Slice the baguette and toast it lightly.
2. Spread a thin layer of mayonnaise on the inside of the bread.
3. Layer the pork, pickled vegetables, cilantro, and cucumber on the sandwich.
4. Drizzle with a little soy sauce and sriracha for an extra kick.
5. Close the sandwich and serve.

Turkey, Brie, and Apple Sandwich

Ingredients:

- 2 slices multigrain or whole wheat bread
- 4-5 slices roasted turkey breast
- 2 slices Brie cheese
- 1/4 apple, thinly sliced (such as Granny Smith)
- Honey mustard or Dijon mustard

Instructions:

1. Spread mustard on one slice of bread.
2. Layer turkey slices, Brie cheese, and apple slices on top.
3. Top with the second slice of bread.
4. Serve as is, or grill the sandwich for a warm, melty version.

Roasted Beet and Goat Cheese Sandwich

Ingredients:

- 2 slices sourdough bread
- 1/2 cup roasted beets, sliced
- 2 ounces goat cheese, crumbled
- Arugula or spinach leaves
- Balsamic glaze or vinaigrette

Instructions:

1. Toast the slices of sourdough bread.
2. Layer the roasted beets, crumbled goat cheese, and greens on one slice of bread.
3. Drizzle with balsamic glaze or vinaigrette for extra flavor.
4. Top with the second slice of bread and serve.

Crispy Chicken and Coleslaw Sandwich

Ingredients:

- 1 chicken breast, breaded and fried
- 1 sandwich bun (such as brioche or toasted hamburger bun)
- 1/2 cup coleslaw (store-bought or homemade)
- Pickles (optional)

Instructions:

1. Cook the breaded chicken breast until crispy and golden.
2. Toast the sandwich bun.
3. Place the crispy chicken on the bottom bun, top with coleslaw and pickles.
4. Close with the top bun and serve.

BBQ Jackfruit Sandwich (Vegan Pulled Pork)

Ingredients:

- 1 can young green jackfruit in brine (drained and shredded)
- 1/2 cup BBQ sauce
- 1 sandwich bun
- Coleslaw (optional)
- Pickles (optional)

Instructions:

1. Shred the jackfruit and sauté in a pan until tender.
2. Stir in BBQ sauce and cook for an additional 5-10 minutes until well coated and heated through.
3. Toast the sandwich bun.
4. Pile the BBQ jackfruit onto the bun and top with coleslaw and pickles if desired.
5. Close the sandwich and serve.

Grilled Shrimp Po' Boy Sandwich

Ingredients:

- 1 sub roll or baguette
- 1/2 pound shrimp, peeled and deveined
- 1 tablespoon Cajun seasoning
- 1 tablespoon olive oil
- Lettuce leaves
- Sliced tomato
- 2 tablespoons remoulade sauce (or mayo with hot sauce)

Instructions:

1. Toss shrimp with Cajun seasoning and olive oil, then grill until cooked through (about 2-3 minutes per side).
2. Toast the sub roll or baguette.
3. Spread remoulade sauce on both sides of the bread.
4. Layer grilled shrimp, lettuce, and tomato on the roll.
5. Close the sandwich and serve.

Sweet and Spicy Meatball Sandwich

Ingredients:

- 1 sub roll or Italian baguette
- 4-5 meatballs (cooked)
- 1/4 cup marinara sauce
- 1 tablespoon honey or maple syrup
- 1 tablespoon sriracha or hot sauce
- 1/4 cup mozzarella cheese, shredded

Instructions:

1. Warm the meatballs in marinara sauce, mixing in honey and sriracha for sweetness and heat.
2. Toast the sub roll.
3. Layer the meatballs and sauce on the roll, then sprinkle mozzarella cheese on top.
4. Broil for a few minutes to melt the cheese.
5. Serve hot.

Veggie and Hummus Wrap

Ingredients:

- 1 large flour tortilla
- 1/4 cup hummus (any flavor)
- 1/2 cup mixed veggies (such as bell peppers, cucumber, carrot, and spinach)
- 1 tablespoon feta cheese (optional)
- Fresh herbs (optional)

Instructions:

1. Spread hummus evenly over the flour tortilla.
2. Layer the mixed veggies, feta, and fresh herbs on top.
3. Roll up the tortilla tightly, folding in the sides to secure the filling.
4. Slice and serve.

Shrimp Avocado Sandwich

Ingredients:

- 2 slices whole-grain or sourdough bread
- 1/2 pound shrimp, cooked and peeled
- 1/2 avocado, sliced
- 1 tablespoon mayonnaise or aioli
- Fresh cilantro leaves
- Lemon wedges for serving

Instructions:

1. Toast the bread slices lightly.
2. Spread mayonnaise or aioli on one slice of bread.
3. Layer the cooked shrimp and avocado slices on top.
4. Garnish with fresh cilantro and a squeeze of lemon juice.
5. Top with the second slice of bread and serve.

Roasted Turkey and Spinach Pita

Ingredients:

- 1 whole wheat pita
- 1/2 cup roasted turkey slices
- 1/4 cup fresh spinach leaves
- 2 tablespoons hummus or Dijon mustard
- Sliced cucumber (optional)

Instructions:

1. Cut the pita in half to create a pocket.
2. Spread hummus or mustard inside the pita.
3. Stuff the pita with turkey slices, spinach, and optional cucumber.
4. Serve immediately or wrap it for an easy lunch.

Grilled Veggie and Goat Cheese Sandwich

Ingredients:

- 2 slices multigrain or sourdough bread
- 1/2 cup assorted grilled vegetables (zucchini, bell peppers, eggplant, etc.)
- 2 ounces goat cheese
- Olive oil for drizzling
- Fresh basil leaves (optional)

Instructions:

1. Grill or sauté the vegetables until tender.
2. Toast the bread slices and drizzle with a little olive oil.
3. Layer the grilled veggies and goat cheese on the bread.
4. Top with fresh basil leaves if desired, then close the sandwich and serve.

Salmon Salad Sandwich

Ingredients:

- 2 slices whole-grain or rye bread
- 1/2 cup cooked and flaked salmon
- 2 tablespoons mayonnaise or Greek yogurt
- 1 tablespoon Dijon mustard
- Chopped celery and red onion (optional)
- Fresh dill for garnish

Instructions:

1. Mix the flaked salmon with mayonnaise, Dijon mustard, celery, and red onion.
2. Spread the salmon salad mixture on one slice of bread.
3. Garnish with fresh dill.
4. Top with the second slice of bread and serve.

Brie, Pear, and Arugula Sandwich

Ingredients:

- 2 slices baguette or sourdough bread
- 2 ounces Brie cheese
- 1 pear, thinly sliced
- A handful of arugula
- Honey (optional)

Instructions:

1. Toast the bread lightly.
2. Spread Brie cheese on one slice of bread.
3. Layer the pear slices and arugula on top of the Brie.
4. Drizzle with a little honey if desired.
5. Top with the second slice of bread and serve.

Cucumber and Cream Cheese Sandwich

Ingredients:

- 2 slices white or whole-wheat bread
- 1/4 cup cream cheese, softened
- 1/2 cucumber, thinly sliced
- Fresh dill or chives for garnish (optional)

Instructions:

1. Spread a thin layer of cream cheese on both slices of bread.
2. Layer the cucumber slices evenly on one slice of bread.
3. Garnish with fresh dill or chives if desired.
4. Close the sandwich, slice, and serve.

Chicken and Waffle Sandwich

Ingredients:

- 2 small waffles (store-bought or homemade)
- 1/2 cup cooked chicken breast, sliced or shredded
- 1 tablespoon maple syrup
- 1 tablespoon hot sauce (optional)

Instructions:

1. Toast the waffles until golden and crispy.
2. Layer the chicken on one waffle, drizzle with maple syrup, and add hot sauce if desired.
3. Top with the second waffle.
4. Serve with additional syrup for dipping.

Veggie and Avocado Wrap

Ingredients:

- 1 large whole-wheat or spinach tortilla
- 1/2 avocado, mashed
- 1/2 cup mixed vegetables (such as bell peppers, cucumber, and spinach)
- 1 tablespoon hummus or tahini
- Lemon juice for drizzling

Instructions:

1. Spread hummus or tahini on the tortilla.
2. Layer mashed avocado and mixed veggies on top.
3. Drizzle with a little lemon juice.
4. Roll the tortilla tightly and slice into halves for serving.

Ham, Egg, and Cheese Croissant Sandwich

Ingredients:

- 1 croissant
- 1 slice ham
- 1 egg
- 1 slice cheese (cheddar, Swiss, or your choice)
- Butter or olive oil for cooking

Instructions:

1. Split the croissant in half and toast lightly.
2. Heat a little butter or oil in a skillet and fry the egg to your desired doneness.
3. Place the ham slice in the skillet to warm it up for a few seconds.
4. Once the egg is cooked, assemble the sandwich by placing the ham, egg, and cheese inside the croissant.
5. Close the sandwich and serve immediately.

Chicken and Pesto Panini

Ingredients:

- 2 slices ciabatta or baguette bread
- 1 grilled chicken breast, sliced
- 2 tablespoons pesto sauce
- 2 slices mozzarella cheese
- Olive oil for grilling

Instructions:

1. Preheat a panini press or grill pan.
2. Spread pesto sauce on one side of each slice of bread.
3. Layer the chicken slices and mozzarella on one slice of bread.
4. Top with the second slice of bread, pesto side down.
5. Brush the outside of the sandwich with olive oil and grill in the panini press until golden brown and crispy.
6. Serve hot.

Buffalo Cauliflower Wrap

Ingredients:

- 1 large whole-wheat or spinach tortilla
- 1 cup roasted cauliflower, tossed in buffalo sauce
- 1/4 cup shredded lettuce
- 1/4 cup shredded carrots
- 2 tablespoons ranch or blue cheese dressing

Instructions:

1. Warm the tortilla in a pan or microwave.
2. Place the roasted buffalo cauliflower in the center of the tortilla.
3. Add the shredded lettuce and carrots on top of the cauliflower.
4. Drizzle with ranch or blue cheese dressing.
5. Fold in the sides of the tortilla and roll it up tightly.
6. Slice in half and serve.

Apple and Cheddar Sandwich

Ingredients:

- 2 slices whole-grain or sourdough bread
- 1/2 apple, thinly sliced
- 2 ounces sharp cheddar cheese
- A drizzle of honey (optional)

Instructions:

1. Toast the bread slices lightly.
2. Layer the apple slices and cheddar cheese on one slice of bread.
3. Drizzle with a little honey if desired for extra sweetness.
4. Top with the second slice of bread and serve.

Bacon, Lettuce, and Tomato Sandwich (BLT)

Ingredients:

- 2 slices toasted bread (white, whole-wheat, or sourdough)
- 4-5 slices cooked bacon
- 2-3 slices tomato
- A few leaves of lettuce
- Mayonnaise (optional)

Instructions:

1. Toast the bread slices to your desired crispness.
2. Spread mayonnaise on one slice of bread (optional).
3. Layer the cooked bacon, tomato slices, and lettuce on the bread.
4. Top with the second slice of bread and serve immediately.

Sweet Chili Chicken Sandwich

Ingredients:

- 2 slices of sandwich bread (your choice)
- 1 grilled chicken breast, sliced
- 2 tablespoons sweet chili sauce
- 1 slice lettuce
- 1 slice tomato
- 1 tablespoon mayonnaise (optional)

Instructions:

1. Toast the bread slices to your desired crispness.
2. Coat the sliced chicken with sweet chili sauce.
3. Layer the lettuce and tomato on one slice of bread.
4. Add the sweet chili chicken on top and spread mayonnaise if using.
5. Close the sandwich with the second slice of bread and serve.

Roasted Garlic and Tomato Sandwich

Ingredients:

- 2 slices of whole-grain or sourdough bread
- 1-2 cloves roasted garlic
- 2-3 slices fresh tomato
- 1 tablespoon olive oil
- Salt and pepper to taste
- Fresh basil leaves (optional)

Instructions:

1. Toast the bread slices lightly.
2. Spread the roasted garlic onto one side of each slice of bread.
3. Layer the tomato slices on top of the garlic.
4. Drizzle with olive oil and season with salt and pepper.
5. Add fresh basil leaves if desired, top with the second slice of bread, and serve.

Mediterranean Veggie Wrap

Ingredients:

- 1 large whole-wheat tortilla
- 1/4 cup hummus
- 1/4 cup cucumber, sliced
- 1/4 cup roasted red pepper, sliced
- 1/4 cup Kalamata olives, sliced
- 1/4 cup feta cheese, crumbled
- A handful of spinach or mixed greens

Instructions:

1. Lay the tortilla flat and spread a thin layer of hummus on it.
2. Arrange the cucumber, roasted red pepper, olives, feta, and spinach in the center.
3. Roll up the tortilla tightly, folding in the sides as you go.
4. Slice in half and serve immediately.

Grilled Cheese with Fig Jam and Prosciutto

Ingredients:

- 2 slices sourdough or rustic bread
- 2 tablespoons fig jam
- 2 slices prosciutto
- 2 slices sharp cheddar cheese
- Butter for grilling

Instructions:

1. Spread a thin layer of fig jam on one side of each slice of bread.
2. Layer the prosciutto and cheese on one slice of bread, fig jam side up.
3. Top with the second slice of bread, fig jam side down.
4. Butter the outside of the sandwich and grill it in a pan over medium heat until golden brown and the cheese is melted.
5. Serve hot.

Hummus and Avocado Toast Sandwich

Ingredients:

- 2 slices whole-grain or sourdough bread
- 1/2 avocado, mashed
- 2 tablespoons hummus
- A sprinkle of chili flakes or lemon zest (optional)
- Salt and pepper to taste

Instructions:

1. Toast the bread slices to your desired crispness.
2. Spread hummus on one slice of toast and mashed avocado on the other.
3. Season with salt, pepper, and chili flakes or lemon zest if desired.
4. Put the slices together to form a sandwich and serve.

www.ingramcontent.com/pod-product-compliance
Lightning Source LLC
LaVergne TN
LVHW061954070526
838199LV00060B/4107